This Troubled World

To
Mrs. Carrie Chapman Catt
who has led so many of us in the struggle for peace

This Troubled World

by Eleanor Roosevelt

Table of Contents

The Case as it Stands

The newspapers these days are becoming more and more painful. I was reading my morning papers on the train not so long ago, and looked up with a feeling of desperation. Up and down the car people were reading, yet no one seemed excited.

To me the whole situation seems intolerable. We face today a world filled with suspicion and hatred. We look at Europe and see a civil war going on, with other nations participating not only as individual volunteers, but obviously with the help and approval of their governments. We look at the Far East and see two nations, technically not at war, killing each other in great numbers.

Every nation is watching the others on its borders, analyzing its own needs and striving to attain its ends with little consideration for the needs of its neighbors. Few people are sitting down dispassionately to go over the whole situation in an attempt to determine what present conditions are, or how they should be met.

We know, for instance, that certain nations today need to expand because their populations have increased. Certain people will tell you that the solution of this whole question lies in the acceptance or rejection of birth control. That may be the solution for the future, but we can do nothing in that way about the populations that now exist. They are on this earth, and modern science has left us only a few places where famine or flood or disease can wipe out large

This Troubled World

numbers of superfluous people in one fell swoop. For this reason certain nations need additional territory to which part of their present populations may be moved; other nations need more land on which to grow necessary raw materials; or perhaps they may need mineral deposits which are not to be found in their own country. You will say that these can be had by trade. Yes, but the nations possessing them will frequently make the cost too high to the nations which need them.

It is not a question today of the "free" interchange of goods. If standards of living were approximately the same, throughout the world, competition would be on an equal basis and then there might be no need for tariffs. However, standards of living vary. The nations with higher standards have set up protective barriers which served them well when they were self-contained, but not so well when they reached a point where they either wished to import or export.

When you take all these things into consideration, the size of this problem is apt to make you feel that even an attempt to solve it in the future by education is futile. Faint heart, however, ne'er won fair lady, nor did it ever solve world problems!

Peace plan after peace plan has been presented to me; most of them, I find, are impractical, or not very carefully thought out. In nearly all of them some one can find a flaw. I have come to look at them now without the slightest hope of finding one full-fledged plan, but I keep on looking in the hope of finding here and there some small suggestion that may be acceptable to enough people to insure an honest effort being made to study it and evaluate its possible benefits.

For instance, one lady of my acquaintance brought me a plan this past spring which sounded extremely plausible. Her premises are: We never again wish to send our men overseas; we wish to have adequate defense; we do not need a navy if we do not intend to go beyond our own shores; submarines and airplanes can defend our shores, with guns along our coasts as an added protection. Therefore, we do not need an army, for our men are going to stay at home. With our coast defenses strong, nobody will land here, so why go to the expense of an army? We do not need battleships or, in fact, any navy beyond submarines because we do not intend to own any outlying possessions.

In this way, said the lady, we will save vast sums of money which can be applied to all the social needs of the day—better housing, better schools, old age pensions, workmen's compensation, care of the blind and crippled and other dependents. There is no limit to what we might do with this money which we now spend on preparation for destruction.

It is a very attractive picture and I wish it were all as simple as that, but it seems to be fairly well proved that guns along our coasts are practically useless. No one, as far as I know, has ever devised an adequate defense by submarines and airplanes, or calculated whether the cost of the development of these two forces would really be any less than what we spend at present on our army and navy.

The greatest defense value of the navy is that its cruising radius is great enough to allow it to contact an attacking force long before that force reaches our shores. If we trusted solely to submarines and airplanes we would have to have them in sufficient number really to cover all our borders, and this type of defense would seem to be almost prohibitive in cost for a nation with a great many miles of border to defend.

Has any one sounded out the people of this country as to their willingness to wait until an attacking enemy comes within the cruising radius of our planes and submarines? Have we faced the fact that this would mean allowing an attacking enemy to come unmolested fairly near to our shores and would make it entirely possible for them to land in a nearby country which might be friendly to them, without any interference on our part? Have our citizens been asked if they are willing to take the risk of doing without trained men? We have always had a small trained army forming the first line of defense in case somebody does land on our borders, or attempts to approach us by land through a neighboring country. Our army has not been thought of as an attacking force; do we want to do away with it?

Are all the people in this country willing also to give up the outlying islands which have come into our possession? Some of them cost us more than they bring in, but others bring certain of our citizens a fair revenue. Can we count on those citizens to accept the loss of these revenues in the interests of future peace?

Perhaps this is part of what we will have to make up our minds to pay some day as the price of peace; but has any one as yet put it in concrete form to the American people and asked their opinion about it?

One of the things that is most frequently harped upon is the vast sums of money spent for war preparation in this country. Very frequently the statements are somewhat misleading. It is true that in the past few years we have spent more than we have for a number of preceding years because we had fallen behind in our treaty strength but, in a world which is arming all around us, it is necessary to keep a certain parity and these expenditures should be analyzed with a little more care than is usual.

For instance, few people realize that in the army appropriation is included all the work done under the army engineers on rivers and harbors, on flood control, etc. One other consideration which is frequently overlooked is that, because of the higher wages paid for labor in this country, whatever we build costs us more than it does in the other nations. One significant fact is that we only spend twelve percent of our national income on our army and navy, as against anywhere from thirty-five to fifty-five percent of the national income spent by nations in the rest of the world. It is well for us to realize these facts and not to feel that our government is doing something that will push us into a position which is incompatible with a desire for peace. We are the most peace loving nation in the world and we are not doing anything at present which would change that situation.

One very intelligent friend of mine developed an idea the other day which seems to me common sense for the present time, at least. "Why do we talk," she asked, "about peace? Why don't we recognize the fact that it is normal and natural for differences to exist? Almost every family, no matter how close its members may be, is quarrelsome at times." Quarrelsome may be too strong a word, so we might better say that differences of opinion arise in the family as to conduct or as to likes and dislikes. Why should we expect therefore, that nations will not have these same differences and quarrels? Why do we concentrate on urging them not to have any differences? Why don't we simply accept the fact that differences always come up and concentrate on evolving some kind of machinery by which the differences may be recognized and some plan of compromise be worked out to satisfy, at least in part, all those concerned? Compromises, of course, have to be made; they are made in every family. There are usually some members of a family, who, by common consent, are the arbitrators of questions that arise, and who hold the family together, or bring them together if relationships become strained.

Ultimate Objectives

What are our ultimate objectives and how shall we achieve them? First, the most important thing is that any difficulties arising should automatically go before some body which will publish the facts to the world at large and give public opinion an opportunity to make a decision. Then, a group of world representatives will have to decide with whom the fault lies. If their decision is not accepted by the nations involved and either nation attempts to use force in coercing the other nation, or nations—in opposition to what is clearly the majority opinion of the world—then and then only, it seems to me, the decision will be made that15 the nation using force is an aggressor nation. Being an aggressor, the majority of nations in opposition would be obliged to resort to some method designed to make that nation realize that they could not with impunity flout the public opinion of the majority.

We need to define what an aggressor nation is. We need to have a tribunal where the facts in any case may be discussed, and the decision made before the world, as to whether a nation is an aggressor or not. Then the steps decided upon could be taken in conjunction with other nations.

First of all, trade should be withdrawn from that nation and they should be barred as traders in the countries disagreeing with them. It would not seem probable that more than this economic weapon would have to be used but, if necessary in the end, the police force could be called upon.

In the case of a clearly defined issue where the majority of nations agreed, the police force would simply try to prevent bloodshed and aggression, and it would be in a very different position from an army which was attempting to attack a country and subjugate it. Even the use of a police force, which so many think of as tantamount to war, would really be very different and there would be no idea of marching into a country or making the people suffer or taking anything from them. It would simply be a group of armed men preventing either of the parties to a quarrel from entering into a real war.

Of course, I can imagine cases in which the police force might find itself in an unenviable position, with two countries engaged in a heated quarrel trying to do away with the police so they could get at each other!

All we can hope is that this situation will not arise and that the non-aggressor party to the quarrel, at least, may be willing to sit peacefully by and see the police force repulse the enemy without wishing to turn into aggressors themselves.

With all our agitation about peace, we lose sight of the fact that with the proper machinery it is easier to keep out of situations which lead to war than it is to bring about peace once war is actually going on.

I doubt very much whether peace is coming to us either through plans, even my own as I have outlined it, or through any of the theories or hopes we now hold. What I have outlined is not real peace, just a method of trying to deal with our difficulties a little better than we have in the past, in the world as it is today. We may, of course, be wiped off the face of the earth before we do even this.

Eleanor Roosevelt

Our real ultimate objective must be a change in human nature for I have, as I said, yet to see a peace plan which is really practical and which has been thought through in every detail. Therefore, I am inclined to believe that there is no perfect and complete program for bringing about peace in the world at the present moment.

I often wonder as I look around the world whether any of us, even we women, really want peace. Women should realize better than any one else, that the spirit of peace has to begin in the relationship between two individuals. They know that a child alone may be unhappy because he is alone, but there will be no quarreling until another child appears on the scene, and then the fur will fly, if each of them desires the same thing at the same time.

Women have watched this for generations and must know, if peace is going to come about in the world, the way to start is by getting a better understanding between individuals. From this germ a better understanding between groups of people will grow.

In spite of this knowledge, I am sure that women themselves are among the worst offenders when it comes to petty quarrels. Mrs. J—— will refuse to speak to Mrs. C—— because Mrs. C——'s dog came through the hedge and mussed up Mrs. J——'s flowerbed. No one will deny that occurrences of this kind are irritating in the extreme, but is it worth a feud between two neighbors, perhaps old friends or even acquaintances who must live next door to each other and see each other almost every day?

At the moment we, as a nation, are looking across the Atlantic and the Pacific, patting ourselves on the back and saying how fortunate we are to be away from all their excitements. We feel a little self-righteous, and forget that we ourselves have been engaged in a war on the average of every forty years since our nation was founded. We even fought a civil war, complicated by the alignment of other nations with one side or the other, though no foreign soldiers actually came to fight on either side.

The people who settled in New England came here for religious freedom, but religious freedom to them meant freedom only for their kind of religion. They were not going to be any more liberal to others who differed with them in this new country, than others had been with them in the countries from which they came. This attitude seems to be our attitude in many situations today.

Very few people in any nation today are inclined to be really liberal in allowing real freedom to other individuals. Like our forebears we want freedom for ourselves, but not for those who differ from us. To think and act as we please within the limits, of course, caused by the necessity for respecting the equal rights which must belong to our neighbors, would seem to be almost a platitudinous doctrine, yet we would frequently like to overlook these limits and permit no freedom to our neighbors. If this is our personal attitude, it is not strange that our national attitude is similar. We are chiefly concerned with the rights and privileges of our own people and we show little consideration for the rights and privileges of others. In this we are not very different from other nations both in the past and in the present.

I can almost count on the fingers of one hand the people whom I think are real pacifists. By that I mean, the people who are really making an effort in their personal lives to bring about an atmosphere which will be conducive to a solution of all our difficulties in a peaceful manner.

The first step towards achieving this end is self-discipline and self-control. The second is a certain amount of imagination which will enable us to understand situations in which other people find themselves. We may learn to be less indignant at any slight or

18

seeming slight, and we may try to find some way by which to remove the cause of the troubles which arise between individuals, if we become disciplined and cultivate our imaginative faculties. Once we achieve a technique by which we control our own emotions, we certainly will be better able to teach young people how to get on together. They may then find some saner way of settling questions under dispute than by merely punching each other's noses!

When we once control ourselves and submit personal differences to constituted authorities for settlement, we can say that we have a will to peace between individuals. Before we come to the question of what may be the technique between nations, however, we must go a step farther and set our national house in order. On every hand we see today miniature wars going on between conflicting interests. As the example most constantly before us, take capital and labor. If their difficulties are settled by arbitration and no blood is shed, we can feel we have made real strides towards approaching our international problems. We are not prepared to do this, however, when two factions in a group having the same basic interests cannot come to an agreement between themselves. Their ability to obtain what they desire is greatly weakened until they can reach an understanding and work as a unit. The basis of this understanding should not be hard to reach if the different personalities involved could forget themselves as individuals and think only of the objectives in view, and of the best way to obtain them.

Granted that they are able to do this, then we can approach our second problem with the knowledge that more deeply conflicting interests are at stake but that those with common interests can state their case so the public may form their opinion. Here again, if you could take it for granted that on both sides a real desire existed amongst those representing divergent interests to consider unselfishly ultimate goals and benefits for the majority, rather than any individual gain or loss, it would undoubtedly be possible to reach a peaceful agreement.

Human beings, however, do not stride from peak to peak, they climb laboriously up the side of the mountain. The public will have to understand each case as it comes up and force divergent interests to find a solution. The real mountain climber never gives up until he has reached the highest peak and the lure of the climb to this peak is always before him to draw him on.

That should be the way in human progress—a peaceful, quiet progress. We cannot follow this way, however, until human nature becomes less interested in self, acquires some of the vision and persistence of the mountain climber, and realizes that physical forces must be harnessed and controlled by disciplined mental and spiritual forces.

When we have achieved a nation where the majority of the people is of this type, then we can hope for some measure of success in changing our procedure when international difficulties arise.

What we have said really means that we believe in one actual way to peace—making a fundamental change in human nature. Over and over again people will tell you that that is impossible. I cannot see why it should be impossible when the record of history shows so many changes already gone through.

Only the other day I heard it stated that there are only two real divisions which can be made between people—the people who have good intentions, and the people who have evil intentions. The same man who made this distinction between people, made the suggestion that eventually there should be in the government, a department where business—the business that wishes to be fair and square—could lay its plans before a chosen group of men representing business, the public and the government. They could ask for advice as to whether the plans proposed were according to the best business interests of the country and the majority of the people and receive in return a disinterested, honest opinion. Immediately the remonstrance was made that this would be impossible because it would be difficult for an advisory group to know if the plans laid before them were honestly stated, and people of evil intentions could use such a group to promote plans for selfish interests rather than for the general welfare. This is undoubtedly true, and we are up against exactly the same situation in trying to obtain peace between groups within nations as we are on the international fronts.

Human beings either must recognize the fact that what serves the people as a whole serves them best as individuals and, through selfish or unselfish interests, they become people of good intentions and honesty. If not we will be unable to move forward except as we have moved in the past with recourse to force, and constant, suspicious watchfulness on the part of individuals and groups towards each other. The preservation of our civilization seems to demand a permanent change of attitude and therefore every effort should be bent towards bringing about this change in human nature through education. This is a slow way and, in the meantime, we need not sit with folded hands and feel that no steps can be taken to ward off the dangers which constantly beset us.

Immediate Steps

We can begin, and begin at once, to set up some machinery. Our international difficulties will then automatically be taken up before they reach the danger point. One of our great troubles is that it is nobody's business to try to straighten out difficulties between nations in the early stages. If they are allowed to continue too long, they grow more and more bitter and little things, which might at first have been easily explained or settled, take on the proportions of a bitter and important quarrel.

We do not scrap our whole judicial machinery just because we are not sure that the people who appear before the bar are telling the truth. We go ahead and do our best to ascertain the truth in any given case, and substantial justice seems to be done in a majority of situations. This same thing would have to satisfy us for a time at least in the results achieved by whatever machinery we set up to solve our international difficulties.

I am not advocating any particular machinery. The need seems fairly obvious. To say that we cannot find a way is tantamount to acknowledging that we are going to watch our civilization wipe itself off the face of the earth.

For those of us who remember the World War, there is little need to paint a picture of war conditions, but the generation that participated in that war is growing older. To the younger group what they have not seen and experienced themselves actually means little.

I heard a gentleman who loves adventure say the other day that he could recruit an army of young people at any time to go to war in any part of the world. They would believe that the danger was slight, and the fun and comradeship and adventure would be attractive. I protested violently that youth today was not so gullible, but down in the bottom of my heart I am a little apprehensive. Therefore, it seems to me that one of our first duties is constantly to paint for young people a realistic picture of war. You cannot gainsay the assertion that war brings out certain fine qualities in human nature. People will make sacrifices which they would not make in the ordinary course of existence. War will give opportunities for heroism which do not arise in every-day living, but this is not all that war will do.

It will place men for weeks under conditions which are physically so bad that years later they may still be suffering from the effects of this "period of adventure" even though they may not have been injured by shot or shell during this time of service. Upon many people it will have mental or psychological effects which will take them years to overcome. In many countries of the world there are people to attest to the changed human beings who have returned to them after the World War. Men who could no longer settle down to their old work, men who had seen such horrors that they could no longer sleep quietly at night, men who do not wish to speak of their experiences. It is a rather exceptional person who goes through a war and comes out unscathed physically, mentally or morally.

Secondly, it is one's duty to youth to point out that there are ways of living heroically during peace times. I do not imagine that Monsieur and Madame Curie ever felt the lack of adventure in their lives, for there is nothing more adventurous than experimentation with an unknown element. Their purpose was to find something of benefit to the human race. They jeopardized no lives but their own.

I doubt if Father Damien ever felt that his life lacked adventure; and I can think of a hundred places in our own country today where men or women might lead their lives unknown or unsung beyond the borders of their own communities and yet never lack for adventure and interest. Those who set themselves the task of making their communities into places in which the average human being may obtain a share, not only of greater physical well-being, but of wider mental and spiritual existence, will lead an active and adventurous life to reach their goal.

This will need energy, patience and understanding beyond the average, qualities of leadership to win other men to their point of view, unselfishness and heroism, for they may be asked to make great sacrifices. To reach their objectives they may have to hand over their leadership to other men, their characters may be maligned, their motives impugned, but they must remain completely indifferent if only in the end they achieve their objectives. Moral courage of a rare kind will be required of them.

In the wars of the past, deeds of valor and heroism have won decorations from governments and the applause of comrades in arms, but the men who lead in civic campaigns may hope for none of these recognitions. The best that can happen to them is that they may live to see a part of their dreams come true, they may keep a few friends who believe in them and their own consciences may bring them inner satisfactions.

Making our every-day living an adventure is probably our best safeguard against war. But there are other steps which we might well take.

This Troubled World

Let us examine again, for example, the ever-recurring question of the need for armaments as a means of defense and protection and see if something cannot be done immediately. Many people feel the building of great military machines lead us directly into war for when you acquire something it is always a temptation to use it.

It is perfectly obvious, however, that no nation can cut down its army and navy and armaments in general when the rest of the world is not doing the same thing.

We ourselves have a long unfortified border on the north which has remained undefended for more than a hundred years, a shining example of what peace and understanding between two nations can accomplish. But we also have two long coast lines to defend and the Panama Canal, which in case of war must be kept open, therefore it behooves us to have adequate naval defense. Just what we mean by adequate defense is a point on which a great many people differ.

Innumerable civilians have ideas as to what constitutes adequate military preparedness and the people most concerned, our military forces, have even more definite ideas. Many people in the United States feel that we are still rendered practically safe by the expanse of water on our east and west coasts. Some people even feel, like Mr. William Jennings Bryan, that if our nation needed to be defended a million men would spring to arms over night. They forget that a million untrained, unarmed men would be a poor defense. We must concede that our military establishments have probably made a more careful, practical study of the situation than any one else, for they know they would have to be ready for action at once.

Whether we accept the civil or the military point of view on preparedness, we can still move forward. We can continue to try to come to an understanding with other nations on some of the points which lead to bad feeling. We can begin first, perhaps, with the

Eleanor Roosevelt

Central and South American nations and continue later with other nations, to enter into agreements which may lead to the gradual reduction of armaments. If we only agree on one thing at a time, every little step is something to the good. Simply because we have so far not been able to arrive at any agreement is no reason for giving up the attempt to agree. No one has as yet discovered a way to make any of the methods of transportation by which we all travel around the world, absolutely safe, but nobody suggests that we should do away with ships and railroads and airplanes. I feel that the people of various nations can greatly influence their governments and representatives and encourage action along the lines of reduction in arms and munitions.

Every international group that meets must bear in mind that they have an opportunity to create better feeling, but to move forward along this particular front also requires the backing of public opinion at home. This opinion may be formed in many little groups all over the world and may be felt in an ever widening circle of nations until it becomes a formidable force in the world as a whole.

Then there is the matter of private interests involved in the manufacture of arms and munitions. I know there are many arguments advanced against government ownership of the factories making arms and munitions. When you know the story of the part played by certain families in Europe whose business it has been to manufacture arms and munitions, however, you wonder if the arguments advanced against this step are not inspired in large part by those whose interests lie in this particular business?

It is true that a government can lose its perspective for a number of reasons. The need for employment may push them to over-production, as well as fear of their neighbors, and they may manufacture so much that the temptation to use it may be great.

This Troubled World

Some governments today manufacture practically all they need for peace-time purposes and this is a safeguard, but for war-time use, all governments would have to fall back on private manufacturers who could convert their plants easily for the manufacturing of war materials. Some governments today encourage private manufacturers to produce arms and munitions needed in peace time by buying from them, but the great danger lies in the uncontrolled private production which is used for export. The element of private profit is a great incentive towards the increase of this business just as it is in any other business. Governments are not tempted in the same way, for they do not manufacture for export or for profit.

It seems to me that we must trust some one and I think perhaps it is wiser to trust a government than the more vulnerable and easily tempted individual. Besides which, a democracy has it within its power to control any government business and, therefore, the idea that our government should control the manufacture of arms and munitions fills me with no great trepidation.

This control of the manufacture of arms and munitions is a measure which could be undertaken by one government alone. It does not have to wait for all the other governments to concur, and so I believe either in complete government ownership or in the strictest kind of government supervision, allowing such manufacture as will supply our own country but which will not create a surplus for exportation, thus removing the incentive for constantly seeking and creating new markets.

The next step will be the mutual curtailment, very gradually I am sure, of the amount of armaments the world over. This is a difficult step, because it requires not only an agreement on the part of all the nations, but sufficient confidence in each other to believe that, having given their word, they will live up to the spirit of the agreement as well as to the letter of it, and not try cleverly to hide whatever they have done from possible inspectors.

They will not, for instance, destroy a battleship and add a half dozen airplanes, telling the other members to the agreement that they have carried out the promised reduction, but forgetting to mention the additions to some other arm of their military service.

This lack of integrity, or perhaps we should call it more politely the desire to be a little more clever than one's neighbor, is what promotes a constant attitude of suspicion amongst nations. This will exist until we have accomplished a change in human nature and that is why for the present it seems to me necessary to have inspection and policing as well as an agreement.

The objection will be made that in the nations which are not democracies a government might build up a great secret arsenal; but in those countries this could be done today for most of them control the press and all out-going information with an iron hand.

Outside of the democracies, government ownership is a much more serious danger on this account. If all nations were obliged to report their military strength to some central body, and this body was allowed to inspect and vouch for the truth of their statements, then all governments could feel secure against that hidden danger which is now part of the incentive for a constant increase in the defense machinery of every nation.

Here again we are confronted with the need of some machinery to work for peace. I have already stated that I doubt if the present League of Nations could ever be made to serve the purpose for which it was originally intended. This does not mean that I do not believe that we could get together. We might even begin by setting up regional groups in different parts of the world which might eventually amalgamate into a central body. It seems to me almost a necessity that we have some central body as a means of settling our difficulties, with an international police force to enforce its decisions, as long as we have not yet reached the point everywhere of setting force aside.

Joint economic action on the part of a group of nations will undoubtedly be very effective, but it will take time to educate people to a point where they are willing to sacrifice, even temporarily, material gains in the interests of peace, so I doubt whether we can count at once on complete cooperation in the use of an economic boycott. To be a real weapon against any nation wishing to carry on war, it must be well carried out by a great number of nations.

Another small and perhaps seemingly unimportant thing might be done immediately. It might be understood that in war time every one should become a part of the military service and no one should be allowed to make any profit either in increased wages or in increased interest on their capital investment. This might bring about a little more universal interest in peace, and more active interest in the efforts to prevent war whether a man were going to the front or staying at home.

Of course, when we talk of "the front" in connection with future wars, we are taking it for granted that future wars will be much like those of the past, whereas most people believe that future wars will have no fronts. What we hear of Spain and China makes this seem very probable. Gases and airplanes will not be directed only against armed forces, or military centers, they may be used for the breaking of morale in the opposing nation. That will mean shelling of unfortified cities, towns and villages, and the killing of women and children. In fact this means the participation in war of entire populations.

One other element must be considered, namely, the creating of public opinion today. Wars have frequently been declared in the past

30

with the backing of the nations involved because public opinion had been influenced through the press and through other mediums, either by the governments themselves or by certain powerful interests which desired war. Could that be done again today in our own country or have we become suspicious of the written word and the inspired message? I think that as a people we look for motives more carefully than we did in the past but whether issues could be clouded for us is one of the questions that no one can answer until the test comes.

I am inclined to think that if a question as serious as going to war were presented to our nation we would demand facts unvarnished by interpretation. Whether we even in our free democracy could obtain them is another question. Who controls the dissemination of news? Is the press totally, uncompromisingly devoted to the unbiased presentation of all news insofar as possible? Is it possible for groups with special interests to put pressure on the press and on our other means of disseminating information, such as the radio and the screen, and to what extent?

This is an interesting study in every country where people are really interested in good will and peace. If these sources of information are not really free should not the people insist that this be one of our first reforms? Without it we can have no sound basis on which to form our opinions.

These are things we can work for immediately, but some of my friends consider that one point transcends all others and epitomizes the way to "peace."

Summary

We can establish no real trust between nations until we acknowledge the power of love above all other power. We cannot cast out fear and therefore we cannot build up trust. Perfectly obvious and perfectly true, but we are back again to our fundamental difficulty—the education of the individual human being, and that takes time. We cannot sit around a table and discuss our difficulties until we are able to state them frankly. We must feel that those who listen wish to get at the truth and desire to do what is best for all. We must reach a point where we can recognize the rights and needs of others, as well as our own rights and needs.

I have a group of religious friends who claim that the answer to all these difficulties is a great religious revival. They may be right, but great religious revivals which are not simply short emotional upheavals lifting people to the heights and dropping them down again below the place from which they rose, mean a fundamental change in human nature. That change will come to some people through religion, but it will not come to all that way, for I have known many people, very fine people, who had no formal religion. So the change must come to some, perhaps, through a new code of ethics, or an awakening sense of responsibility for their brothers, or a discovery that whether they believe in a future life or not, there are now greater enjoyments and rewards in this world than those which they have envisioned in the past.

I would have people begin at home to discover for themselves the meaning of brotherly love. A friend of mine wrote me the other day that she wondered what would happen if occasionally a member of Congress got up and mentioned in the House the existence of brotherly love. You laugh, it seems fantastic, but this subject will, I am sure, have to be discussed throughout the world for many years before it becomes an accepted rule. We will have to want peace, want it enough to pay for it, pay for it in our own behavior and in material ways. We will have to want it enough to overcome our lethargy and go out and find all those in other countries who want it as much as we do.

Some time we must begin, for where there is no beginning there is no end, and if we hope to see the preservation of our civilization, if we believe that there is anything worthy of perpetuation in what we have built thus far, then our people must turn to brotherly love, not as a doctrine but as a way of living. If this becomes our accepted way of life, this life may be so well worth living that we will look into the future with a desire to perpetuate a peaceful world for our children. With this desire will come a realization that only if others feel as we do, can we obtain the objectives of peace on earth, good will to men.